WARWICK

A Short History & Guide

S U
COU

East Gate.

WARWICK

A Short History & Guide

CHRISTINE M. CLULEY

AMBERLEY

View from St Mary's Tower.

First published 2011

Amberley Publishing
The Hill, Stroud
Gloucestershire GL5 4ER

www.amberley-books.com

Copyright © Christine M. Cluley, 2011

The right of Christine M. Cluley to be identified as the
Author of this work has been asserted in accordance with
the Copyrights, Designs and Patents Act 1988.

ISBN 978 1 4456 0278 3

British Library Cataloguing in Publication Data.
A catalogue record for this book is available from the
British Library.

Typesetting by Amberley Publishing.
Map illustration by User design.
Printed in Great Britain.

CONTENTS

FOREWORD

Christine Cluley's book will be of interest to anyone who lives in Warwick or visits the town. It describes a walking tour around the town which takes in all the sites of major interest and puts each into its own proper historical context. The architectural details of buildings which would normally pass unnoticed are pointed out and explanations given as to why they are there. Readers like myself, who think that they know Warwick well, will revisit the town with fresh eyes. Those visiting for the first time will leave well informed, having had the most interesting places pinpointed and described for them. Much time will have been saved by the choice of route and the reader's interest increased by the commentary given.

Warwick is a beautiful town with a long and interesting history. It is fascinating to read to what extent the fire of 1694 and the regulations imposed to regulate its rebuilding have influenced the appearance of the town as we know it. We are indebted to Christine Cluley for making her knowledge of Warwick available to us.

Martin Dunne, Lord-Lieutenant of Warwickshire

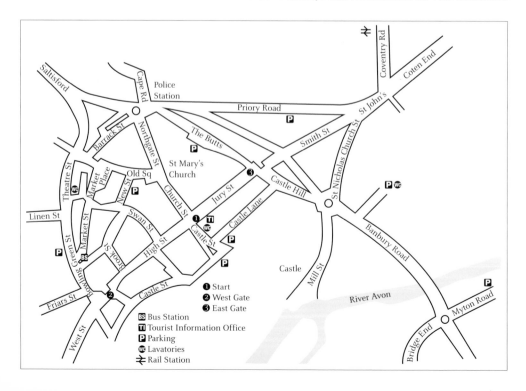

A POTTED HISTORY

Warwick may have originated as a small Saxon settlement by a weir on the River Avon. In AD 914 Ethelfleda, Lady of the Mercians and daughter of King Alfred, established one of her ten new *burhs,* or defended settlements, on the hilltop site overlooking the early settlement. It offered a good defensive stronghold against the Danes who had invaded and occupied land further north, and would provide a safe haven to local people in time of war. The settlement was named *Waerinc Wicum* on a deed of 1001.

The town benefited from the success of the wars against the Danes and it was made the county town of the new shire of Warwickshire. By the time of the Norman Conquest it was a thriving town with its own mint, and in 1086 the Domesday Book recorded 244 dwellings, which may have provided homes for up to 1,500 inhabitants.

In 1068 a wooden motte and bailey castle was built here by William the Conqueror as part of his plan to gain control of the Midlands. He was also responsible for creating the mound, now known as Ethelfleda's Mound.

His son, William Rufus, created the Earldom of Warwick for one of his supporters, Henry Beaumont (1088-1119), who changed his name to Henry de Newburgh. He was appointed Constable of Warwick Castle. The castle was rebuilt in stone from the twelfth century onwards and was complete by about 1250.

Warwick's main prosperity relied on the fact that it was a military garrison and its economy was dependant on the castle. It was not near any main routes and so it was denied a share in long distance trade. There was much competition from other towns with markets and fairs, for example Stratford-upon-Avon and Coventry, so it really only catered for the local populace.

The town's defences at this time would have been an earth rampart, a ditch and a wooden wall surrounding a very small area of buildings comprising the settlement. A stone wall was started but there is no archaeological evidence that it was ever finished. There were three gates, but no foundations have been discovered for the north gate and it is not certain exactly where it was situated.

A bridge was mentioned in 1208 and this allowed the settlement of Bridge End to grow south of the river. Trading must have started in Saxon times but the first documentary evidence of markets dates from the mid-twelfth century, when they were held twice weekly on Wednesday and Saturday. By 1482 the suburbs of Smith Street, Saltisford and West Street were well established. In 1545, Warwick received its first Royal Charter. This assigned certain property of the late College, and of the Guild, to the burgesses of Warwick for certain closely defined objects (mainly the maintenance of the churches). In doing so it created a corporation, but one with very limited powers. The second charter, of 1554, created a proper corporation with much fuller powers.

By the beginning of the seventeenth century the general street pattern was already established, and probably had been from the time of Domesday Book. The houses on

Ethelfleda's Mound.

all the main streets, inside and outside the town defences, were built fairly closely together. There was a social mix of people, with businesses and workshops nestling in close proximity to bigger merchants' houses. Most houses had gardens behind them for growing food and keeping animals. There were shops fronting some of the houses and tradesmen had their workshops behind their homes.

Life in this market town ambled on for several centuries, avoiding any serious dramas or crises. It was fortunate to escape almost unscathed from the civil wars of the seventeenth century, especially as the castle's occupant, Sir Robert Greville, Lord Brooke, sided with the Parliamentarians and put the castle in a state of defence. During his absence, Sir Edward Peyto of Chesterton, with a Parliamentary garrison, was besieged at the castle by the Earl of Northampton, the royalist Lord–Lieutenant of the county. Shots were exchanged and several of Northampton's men were killed. Prisoners taken at Edge Hill and the Battle of Worcester were confined in Caesar's and Guy's Towers and goods plundered from the Royalists after the battle were brought and held at the castle. A governor was appointed in 1643 and a garrison was maintained there until 1660, when Colonel Hawksworth was ordered to disband the garrison and deliver possession of the castle back to Lord Brooke.

Architectural change occurred at a gentle pace. For example, the Market Hall and the Shire Hall – two medieval public buildings – were replaced in the latest seventeenth-century style.

Castle – Caesar's Tower.

Tudor timber framing – Lord Leycester Hospital.

Original colour decoration – Lord Leycester Hospital.

Fulke Greville, fifth Lord Brooke.

By the 1690s, the population had slowly increased to approximately 3,000. This uneventful way of life was shocked into dynamic change as a consequence of a great disaster.

On the afternoon of Wednesday 5 September 1694, the town was nearly destroyed by the Great Fire of Warwick, which probably started in a workshop in the garden of a house in Leycester Place. Fanned by a south-westerly breeze, it spread rapidly along High Street. It continued down as far as the house of Sir Simon Archer – now the Lord Leycester Hotel. The building was set back from the road and the courtyard formed a firebreak, enabling the fire to be stopped from travelling any further. The wind then changed direction, pushing the fire up Church Street as far as the North Gate area and spreading into the Market Place. By the time it died out, the fire had destroyed or damaged 250 houses and shops. The Shire Hall and the Beauchamp Chapel of St Mary's were among the public buildings to escape intact.

Lord Brooke, owner of Warwick Castle and one of the most important aristocrats in the county, together with the local gentry immediately organised help for the sufferers, clearance of the burned areas and plans for the rebuilding. An Act of Parliament set out strict requirements for materials and designs for the new streets and buildings. Masons and surveyors were hired and the work commenced as soon as it was practical.

Most of the rebuilding was complete by the time Celia Fiennes, a redoubtable lady traveller, visited in 1697. She commented that 'the streets are very handsome and the buildings regular and fine...' In 1716 the author Daniel Defoe wrote '... it is now rebuilt in so noble and so beautiful a manner, that few towns in England make so fine an appearance'. The houses were not showy or overstated, reflecting the modest demands of a small county town.

The power of the regulations must have discouraged any alterations to the town for at least one generation. But as the eighteenth century passed, attitudes relaxed and perhaps one or two daring owners, aware of new fashions appearing in other towns, added a little decoration to the outside of their houses. In this way, porch covers, fanlights and balconies appeared as keen followers of fashion refaced the fronts of their houses. One or two bay windows appeared, but this feature was not a popular innovation. The civic authorities also kept up with the Joneses. The Court House was created *c.* 1725–8 and the Shire Hall was replaced in 1758.

As the county town, Warwick was continually busy with a constant stream of people coming in to market, attending the law court and taking part in daily businesses and trades. Four times a year, the regular proceedings of the Assizes drew in even more visitors, who came to see the colourful procession of the judges, leer at the prisoners entering the courts in Shire Hall, and wait with noisy excitement for the verdict. Just as popular were the Quarter Sessions, bringing in all the JPs from around the county, traders, those needing licences for business or leisure, and sightseers who enjoyed watching the minor felons brought to justice.

The crimes brought before the Bench were probably the same heard by JPs in this century all over the country. Richard Chambers, a rogue and vagabond who was wandering and begging without having obtained any legal settlement, was committed to the House of Correction. Robert Wilmot was indicted for using and exercising the trade of a baker without having served seven years as an apprentice. Even men of the cloth appeared before the bench – the Revd Robert Millers maliciously and injuriously broke a window and destroyed the glass windows of the dwelling house of Jane Sparry. Illegal indoor activities were duly reported – Thomas Chadband allowed tippling in his house during the time of divine services on the Lord's Day and John Philpot allowed 'unlawful games to be used in his house'. William Chamberlain's drain was a nuisance and he was ordered to remove it.

That merry monarch Charles II had made horse racing a popular pastime and in 1707 Lord Brooke, another sporting enthusiast, gave £15 'towards making a horse race'. Two years later, the first race took place on St Mary's Common and over three hundred years later, the race meetings are still a popular pastime. Crowds were attracted to the races and the wealthier enthusiasts probably stayed at the various hostelries in the town. No doubt, after the meetings some of the racing fraternity reluctantly attended the court!

As in other towns, entertainment was provided for all tastes. During the race days, balls were held at the Shire Hall and public breakfasts were staged at the Court House. Fox hunting had been introduced into the area and hunt balls added to the day's entertainment. Concerts and card parties also kept the gentry and the more prosperous merchants busy. For those less genteel, there were the usual taverns and gaming houses to relieve customers of their earnings.

Other entertainments included a theatre, built in the 1790s, where such famous names as Charles Kemble, William Charles Macready and Edmund Kean trod the boards. David Garrick also made himself known at the Theatre but obviously found no entertainment to please him when he was not on stage. In a reference to Guy of Warwick, a mythical hero, he sneered,

On Warwick town and castle fair
I've feasted full my wandering eyes;
Where things abound antique and rare
To strike the stranger with surprise.
But if again I e'er appear
On this unsocial lifeless spot
May I be spitted on Guy's spear
Or boiled within his porridge pot.

It is not recorded whether the townspeople took this verse as an insult or admired it as a witty piece. It made no difference, as life in Warwick continued at its gentle pace. It was typical of many other small market towns, conducting commerce with a measured tread, conservative in its politics, with very little disturbing its peace. It remained in this happy state for most of the eighteenth century. Things were rather different just ten miles up the road in Coventry. That had been a prosperous medieval city, its business overseen by rich guilds, and had been at one time the seat of the bishop. Had the bishop sat in Warwick, its status would have been immeasurably enhanced with its castle, priory, courts and collegiate church. Coventry was the cosmopolitan city and Warwick was in danger of becoming a backwater.

Although the inhabitants had much to amuse them, the general impression voiced by George Lipscombe in *A Journey to South Wales* (1799) was that Warwick was characterised by an 'uncommon dullness' and 'air of melancholy, a place remarkable for dull inactivity, and the careless inattention of the inhabitants to all that might obviously contribute to its improvement and its embellishment'. However, another major change was about to be forced on the people of Warwick. Although much less dramatic than the fire, the new bridge across the River Avon had an enormous impact on the town.

By the last decades of the eighteenth century, the old bridge by the castle was in a parlous condition. No one was sure who owned it and therefore who should pay for the repair. Moreover, the second Earl of Warwick (1746-1816) wanted to enlarge his grounds. He made agreements with the Corporation to purchase various pieces of land and paid three quarters of the cost for the building of the bridge 250 yards upstream. It was probably designed by Robert Mylus and built by William Eborall (a Warwick man), and building started in 1789. The Earl then had a wall built across Castle Street and demolished the few houses that were left inside the new grounds. Castle Hill was widened and some streets demolished. From being noisy, busy areas, Mill Street and Bridge End very quickly became quiet neighbourhoods and the traffic in Castle Street was greatly reduced. This probably pleased the owners, as these areas gradually became more gentrified.

Having acquired a great deal more land, the Earl invited the famous landscape gardener Lawrence 'Capability' Brown to landscape it. Correspondence between him and Brown reveals the Earl's opinion of the town folk. He had required Brown to find him another gardener to 'take care of the garden and hothouse, but he must be particularly an extream sober man'. Brown had found one for him on a previous occasion, but although this man was good 'he in a few weeks gott Drunk often and at last fell down the stairs, broke his skull and dyed shockingly. Our town', continued the Earl, 'is enough to debauch anybody that is not already steady and sober by nature.'

The inhabitants whose homes were in the way of the Earl's vision possibly required a stiff drink! They suffered massive disruption as a whole area was flattened and its appearance changed forever. Folk memories of the Great Fire must have been in their thoughts while they made preparations to leave houses that had been in their families for generations. The visual impact was huge. The new road and the walls cut off a familiar view, and may have created a feeling of social division – an early 'them and us'.

This great activity also had dramatic consequences on the life and fortunes of the Earl. It realised his vision of a much larger estate, distancing himself and the castle from the town. But all the wheeling, dealing and spending resulted in his bankruptcy. Some of those who suffered from the change may have thought that it was well deserved.

On 4 January 1806 the first copy of the *Warwick Advertiser* was published. It faithfully reported international, national and local news and kept the citizens up to date with club and association meetings, church services and criminal activities. Of many reports, one must have brought smiles to the readers. On 24 October 1823, a dancing bear and its owner took lodgings in Saltisford for one night – the bear locked in the outhouse. In the night some men broke in and disturbed the bear. It awoke, hugged one of the men, which caused a great commotion, then ran off down the Saltisford and Oil Mill Lane. It met a drunken old woman whom it hugged, and she broke her cup. She ran off to complain to the Watch that she had been hugged by a tall man dressed in black. The bear danced down Smith Street and began to help travellers across the bridge in St John's, and was soon pursued by a large party of police, dogs and amateur hunters. It outran them until finally dogs found it fast asleep in an osier bed. After four hours

George Greville, second Earl of Warwick.

of freedom, the adventurous bear was recaptured having hugged a large number of surprised townspeople.

During the nineteenth century, Warwick's 'upstart rival', Leamington, attracted the nation's attention, with its up-to-date architecture and healing spa waters. The town developed with its Pump Room, its many royal visitors, and its thriving social scene. This can now be seen as a great advantage to Warwick, as developers were very busy two miles east, leaving the town with its older, solid but handsome buildings and streets untouched by the fanciful glamour of Regency style.

Animals were popular visitors to Warwick. In 1825, Mr George Wombwell brought his two lions, Nero and Wallace, to the town. Nero was born 21 January 1820; he was 4 feet 6 inches high, weighed four hundredweight and was valued at £1,000. Two fights were arranged, during which Wallace mauled four dogs and killed two. Admittance was three guineas and they were held in Factory Yard. The cost of the fight was £300 and takings were £350–£400. Gate-crashers were a nuisance and caused fighting to break out. In 1825 the Warwick magistrates were complimented on moving the fight out of town, but criticised for allowing the lion fights to take place.

Warwick is fortunate to have retained so many beautiful buildings. Sometimes, it is providential to be passed by and overlooked by time and to let other towns take the brunt of development. Even though Warwick enjoyed a minor industrial revolution between 1790 and 1828, the centre retained its timeless quality. The opening of the Warwick and Napton Canal in 1800 brought the benefits of a drop in the price of coal and improved communications.

Elephants in Jury Street.

By 1815, the main streets had been culverted, flagged and lighted and the water supply had been improved. William Field wrote in his *History of Warwick* that the town 'could claim to be described as neat, airy and cleanly ... a spacious, regular, handsome and flourishing town'. The suburbs expanded with industries starting up and streets of Victorian houses were built for the workers. The town thrived, with general trade providing necessities and luxuries to a growing population. Some of the wealthier inhabitants invested in Leamington and their profits fuelled the growth of family banks in Warwick.

In 1830 there were fourteen coach routes but when the railway arrived in 1851, there were to be no fast trains. Passengers who wanted express trains had to get to Leamington. Fortunately, in 1881 the Leamington and Warwick Tramway was installed and, with their horse-drawn vehicles, provided the necessary transport from High Street right through to Leamington. Interestingly, elephants were not the usual mode of transport in Warwick! Electricity replaced the horses in 1905 and continued until 1930, when the tramway company operated with motor buses.

By the late 1920s, public transport was competing with private cars on Warwick's historic streets. Motor traffic was causing trouble, and by the 1930s there were long jams on Bank Holidays in summer. Warwick's peace and calm were becoming a distant memory.

Already by the end of the nineteenth century visitors had come to appreciate Warwick's character and charm. The town had become a place on the tourist map. Even Queen Victoria made a public visit in 1858 and stayed at the castle. The castle had been

Window –Aylesford House.

ANOTHER
Lion Fight.

GEO. WOMBWELL
Has the honour of announcing that his

FINE LION,
Wallace,

Is matched to FIGHT SIX DOGS, Two at a time,
for ONE HUNDRED SOVEREIGNS a-side, with
Mr. EDWARDS, *Lombard-Street, Liverpool,*

On Saturday Evening next,

The 30th of JULY, 1825, at Seven o'Clock, in the

FACTORY YARD, WARWICK.

Three of the Dogs engaged in the Fight with Nero,
will be employed on this occasion.

Admittance, ONE SOVEREIGN, HALF-A-
SOVEREIGN, & FIVE SHILLINGS, Back Seats.

[H. SHARPE, PRINTER, WARWICK.

Poster for the Lion Fight – 1825.

Fanlight and Corinthian Columns – Old Square.

Victorian Pargetting – Westgate School.

Market Street – 1930s.

open to individual visitors since the 1690s, and by 1900 there was a permanent ticket office for public visitors with a guide to show them round. In the first decades of the twentieth century, the author J. R. R. Tolkien visited the town and 'found Warwick, its trees, its hill, and its castle, to be a place of remarkable beauty'.

By the 1960s, motor traffic was causing such severe problems that the planners were forced to introduce systems to deal with the twin problems of traffic and parking. One of these was the A46 Warwick Bypass, which must have alleviated the problem to a great extent. From the 1980s housing estates continued the expansion outside the walls.

Warwick had been fortunate not to suffer much damage during the Second World War. However, some areas in the town suffered from the post-war planning fashions, which were being implemented in the late 1940s. So great was the concern that in 1951, The Warwick Society was founded to oppose the knocking down of buildings for road improvements and other things. Some real damage was done to the fabric of Warwick in the 1970s by developers. Market Street is an example of nondescript structures that replaced some of Warwick's older buildings, which could have been improved. Although the people of Warwick challenged the planners, two of the most controversial buildings were allowed – multi-storey car parks – one of which has been proposed as the ugliest building in the Midlands.

However, most of Warwick is still a very attractive, busy market town, popular with residents and visitors. It maintains its importance as the county town of Warwickshire, a thriving community in the heart of England. Warwick Castle is justly famous

The Mill Garden.

throughout the world but the town itself has much to offer the visitor who is willing to explore its attractive streets and discover its unique history.

As you follow this tour, you can make your own mind up about the mixture of tradition and modernity.

THE TOUR

This tour should take approximately two hours, but this does not include visiting buildings.

The tour starts outside the Court House, at the historic crossroads of Church Street, Jury Street, Castle Street and High Street, halfway up the incline between the surviving town gates. To your left is High Street and at the end is Westgate. To your right is Jury Street and at the end is Eastgate. This gives you a good impression of the size of the town where, for over a thousand years, people have lived, worked and gone about their business. In medieval times, a cross stood in the middle of this very busy spot and it was probably a cause of much congestion, especially on Wednesday market days, when butter and cheese were sold around the cross.

Take some time to enjoy one of the best views in Warwick. Looking north up Church Street, you have a delightful vista of the wide, elegant thoroughfare, with St Mary's Collegiate church completing the picture. The view you are now admiring is the result of rebuilding after the fire of 1694, which included the setting out of the square in front of the church. This was once the site of the Wednesday barley market.

In November 1695, King William III stood where you are standing now. He was witness to a very different scene: St Mary's was a shell, its bells melted, and half the town was in ruins after the calamitous fire. However, the bells of St Nicholas' church rang a welcome to His Majesty, and refreshments were distributed at the cross, where a bonfire was lit to mark the occasion. Some may have thought that a bonfire was inappropriate, considering the scenes of the previous year.

The majority of those who planned and rebuilt Warwick were well educated and had some knowledge of the wider world. They had probably visited London – just one of the several towns damaged by fires in the recent past – and had seen the stylish and modern rebuilding. This was their opportunity to display their knowledge. For example, on several buildings on this tour you will see elements of neo-classical architecture. This was a fashionable style that owed its popularity to the wealthy and educated classes. Its use in the rebuilding of Warwick no doubt indicates the social aspirations of the town's leaders.

Several master builders had come to Warwick to offer their services and the officials chose Francis Smith and his brother, William, to work on the church. Francis probably also advised on the architectural style of the rebuilding of the houses. Although he was only a young man at this time, he was no doubt ambitious, with a keen eye to his future, and would have been careful to keep abreast with the latest fashions and the tastes of prospective patrons.

On the corners of the crossroads you can see four very attractive buildings, one of which is the Court House that you are standing outside. The other three are houses, and as they were in such an important location, the officials responsible for the rebuilding wanted them to make a visual statement of style and grandeur. They were built of stone

Aylesford House.

FRANCIS SMITH (1672–1738)
'Smith of Warwick', as he became known, was a
renowned builder who was responsible for dozens of
beautiful houses in the Midlands. He was the third son
of Francis Smith, a building contractor of Tettenhall
Wood, Staffordshire. His elder brother, William, was
appointed one of the three surveyors responsible for
the laying out and designing of Warwick following the
fire. Alongside local craftsman Samuel Dunckley, the
brothers were appointed as masons in overall charge
of the rebuilding of the western half of St Mary's.
It has also been suggested that Smith was a strong
influence behind the design adapted for the main
street frontages. In 1697, Francis built No. 22 Northgate
Street for himself and brought his new wife, Anne
Lea, the daughter of a Warwick merchant to live there
in 1702. Smith was a member of the Corporation and
was mayor in 1713-4 and 1728-29. He was involved in
much work around Warwick, which included being in
charge of maintenance at Warwick Castle. He is buried
in St Mary's Churchyard.

but were rendered with plaster, probably in the Regency period, to reflect the owners' awareness of fashion.

While most other houses in Warwick had two storeys, these were ordered to have three, which certainly gives them an air of confidence. The regulations dictated the basic design: 'the first two stories ten foot each and the third story eight foot high, the garrets as shall hereafter be appointed and directed by the Commissioners', but insisted on a more lavish and individual style of decoration. The decoration on the three houses illustrates the planners' and owners' understanding of classical architecture and their confidence in displaying it.

Aylesford House (opposite) stands on the corner of Castle Street and High Street. It is one of the best examples of late seventeenth-century architecture, with its broken-apex pediment design over the upstairs window overlooking High Street. The window onto Castle Street also has an attractive pediment, and is framed with a repeat pattern. The painted walls, the elegant balconies, the modern windows and front entrance are not original features – sad but necessary modernisation. However, these do not detract too much from the visual perfection. The original owners of this house were Mary and William Savage – Mr Savage was a barber-surgeon. If you look at the top of the drainpipe, you can see their initials and the date of completion (shown overleaf). Further down the drainpipe are three decorative plaques; one depicts a lion and the other two are birds. You will be able to see the splendid front from Church Street in a few moments.

Each of the houses at the crossroads has classical pilasters on it. Aylesford House has Ionic pilasters, which are the second highest of the classical orders – socially, rather than in terms of height! The house opposite, on the west corner of Church Street, also displays the Ionic style. This was the home of Mr Whadcock. He was a merchant, alderman and treasurer, and perhaps to underline his status, his house was more richly decorated than the other two. If you look carefully you can see carved flowers, wreaths and even a cherub's head.

Does the house on the opposite corner seem more or less elegant to you? The lower part of the house seems plainer but at roof level it is lavishly decorated and the builder has used Corinthian pilasters, the most prestigious of the original classical orders. The house belonged to Mr Blisset, who was an alderman and, in 1703–4, Mayor of Warwick. His choice of the highest order may have been a witty reminder of his status in the town. Interestingly, these three owners declined to choose Doric – the lowest order and most simple.

These three houses need to be considered as a set. The designers wanted to demonstrate their intellectual ability, as shown by the different use of capitals, as well as creating a sense of harmony and giving grandeur and status to this important crossroads.

Turn left, cross at the zebra crossing, turn right, then left into Church Street. Stop at a convenient spot.

You can now see the fourth corner building, the Court House (shown on page 25), which is an excellent example of seventeenth-century public architecture. An added distinction is the fact it was built by Francis Smith, whose talent and skills are still reflected in the town today. The Cross Tavern, a timber-framed building, once stood on this corner and its upper room, called the Parlour, was used as the Council Chamber. The Parlour on the first floor, fronting on to Castle Street, was used for corporation hospitality, and was the only part that was damaged by the fire.

By the 1720s, the corporation decided to have a new building to reflect the importance of the Town Council, and to complement the quality of the houses on the three other corners. Smith was probably influenced by the Italian architects of the day and incorporated elements of palazzo design by using raised Doric pilasters and rusticated

Drain head.

Ionic pilasters.

Corinthian pilasters.

The Court House.

masonry. It also has a flat roof – not the wisest architectural feature for an English building! It was completed by 1730 and cost £2,254.

It is a two-storied building of rusticated ashlar masonry. The ground floor has round-headed openings, while on the upper floor the bays are divided by Roman Doric pillars and surmounted by a triglyph frieze, cornice and parapet. A central niche on the Jury Street front contains a figure of Justice by Thomas Stayner, with the Royal Arms above and the badge of the town below. The statue has a secret! It was cast in metal but cleverly made to look like stone.

The four corner buildings have always made a great impression on visitors. Although following the regulations to the letter, the houses exude a joyous air in what was then a most important place in the town. The Court House, more restrained, reflects the dignity of public office. They create a harmonious and pleasing picture.

Turn and walk up 100 yards and stop outside the Zetland Arms,
opposite the Athenaeum.

This elegant, wide street has retained most of its original seventeenth-century character. However, there have been some alterations since the rebuilding.

The Athenaeum and the Old Library to its left were built on the site of four post-fire houses. The façade is a later addition and the style reflects the contemporary fashion for Greek classical architecture that was being popularised by Robert Adam (1728–92). It is an example of owners who wanted to be up to date and the alterations to the post-fire house were probably designed and carried out by William Hiorn or his son, Francis, in the 1780s. The Hiorns were a well-respected family firm of builders native to Warwick.

This building is another example of the use of classical elements. The stone style of the lower part of the wall is called rustication. This is masonry cut in massive blocks with deep joints, giving a sense of strength and authority. The windows are bordered by pilasters with stylised Corinthian capitals to imply status. A pediment tops the central window. A particularly attractive feature is the heart-shaped ironwork in the lunettes – the half-moon-shaped windows. You can see the evidence of the earlier building behind the balustrade.

The Athenaeum was established in 1847 to welcome men from the gentry and middle classes to meet together to discuss matters of the day and to afford 'facilities for moral and intellectual improvement, by the aid of a library, reading, and news room'. The committee may have wished to reflect their affiliation to the London Athenaeum – Athena was the Greek goddess of wisdom and her temple was named the Athenaeum.

The club finally closed its doors in the 1960s and was taken over by Warwick County Council as premises for the library service, incorporating the library that had been established next door in 1866. When the library service moved to Barrack Street in the 1980s, the two buildings were sold to private businesses.

Cross the road and stand by the war memorial.

The cross is based on the style of an Eleanor cross. King Edward I had twelve lavishly decorated stone monuments erected between 1291 and 1294 in memory of his wife, Eleanor of Castille, marking the nightly resting-places along the route taken by her body on the way to London. This model has been used as a war memorial to those who died in the two world wars.

Warwick's cross was unveiled by Lord Algernon Percy on 10 July 1921. It is made of Portland stone surmounting a three-stepped octagonal base. The cross has bronze plaques on its lower levels with the names of the dead. Above the plaques are four shallow niches, and above these are carved shields with the arms of the following towns: Warwick, Leamington, Coventry, Stratford-upon-Avon, Kenilworth, Rugby, Birmingham and Sutton Coldfield. Above the shields are carvings of the symbols connected with the county of Warwickshire: the Swan of Avon, representing William Shakespeare, the Dun Cow, the mythical opponent of Guy of Warwick, the Bear and Ragged Staff, the badge of the Earls of Warwick, and the antelope, which is the badge of the Warwickshire Regiment.

Walk down the narrow passageway behind the war memorial.

As you walked up Church Street, the Collegiate Church of St Mary and its huge tower were in your view. The church existed before the Norman Conquest, and it was established as a college of canons in 1123. Rebuilding began in 1369 and the Beauchamp chapel was added between 1443 and 1462.

Pause a few yards up the path to admire the architecture of the Beauchamp chapel on the right hand end of the building. It looks very different from the other end of the church. The fifteenth-century chapel was built in the medieval style known as Perpendicular. This is an architectural style that favours tall, slender shapes, pushing up to heaven. However, the left hand end of the church was rebuilt after the fire and the style of architecture reflects attempts to imitate or complement the medieval tradition

Athenaeum.

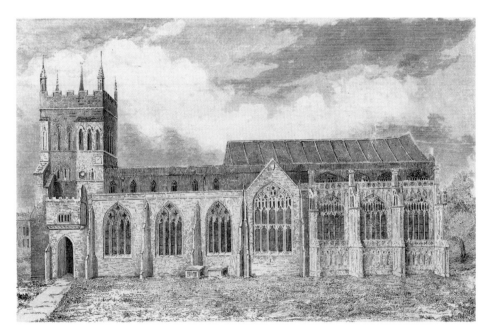

St Mary's before the fire.

– only with an eighteenth-century twist. We will be looking at more of the church shortly.

Continue down the passage to the lamppost and turn left.

The pathway on your right is called the Tink a Tank. There are various explanations for the name, one of which claiming it is a clipped version of 'Think and Thank' – a quick prayer from passers-by. Another version is that it may imitate the sound made by people's footsteps as they hurry along the passage. Tink a Tank leads to The Butts, a road that follows the line of the old wall. You will be able to look down this road later on the tour.

As you walk along, notice the old wall on your right, which may be part of the old college precinct. You will come to a gate in the wall. This leads into the College Gardens, where the building that housed the canons who settled here in 1123 once stood. After the death of Richard Beauchamp in 1439, his chapel was built according to his instructions and at the same time a new college for the Vicars Choral and a new deanery were built and surrounding walls constructed. In 1462 a choir school (cantaria) was added, and was known as the Song School. College life continued uneventfully until the middle of the sixteenth century. Then, King Henry VIII's reform of religious foundations brought the work of the college to an abrupt end in July 1544. The deanery was sold to three Tavener brothers in 1545 and is believed to be the present old vicarage, which has been refaced and lies almost opposite the alleyway called Old Pound.

After that, the site of the school was leased to the King Henry VIII-endowed school and by 1782 only the college building remained. The school continued in this building

The Old College.

until it was sold in 1880 for £1,800 to a solicitor of Lincoln's Inn, London, who had the buildings demolished in 1882. The only materials saved were some timbers, which were used to make a sty for the headmaster's pigs at the new school. The school then moved to the new site at Myton, a small village between Warwick and Leamington. The college site was then bought by the vicar of St Mary's and hired out as a private garden and, later, a tennis court for the King's High School for Girls. The Trustees of St Mary's Church now welcome everyone to spend time here and enjoy the peace.

Continue up the path.

You will notice graffiti carved into the stones – perhaps the pupils who attended the school carved these during their free moments. Unfortunately, they did not include dates!

Exit by the top gate. Turn left. Walk towards the Tower and St Mary's Church.

THE COLLEGIATE CHURCH OF ST MARY

The tower of this beautiful church has been a familiar sight on the skyline for centuries. On close viewing, the church does not disappoint the eager visitor. Unlike the castle, whose presence is felt but unseen, St Mary's Tower can be observed from most places in the town, as well as over the countryside for miles around. The fire destroyed most of the church building, leaving only the fabric of the chancel and the Beauchamp chapel. This may be because Lord Brooke had given orders to save the chapel, perhaps because his ancestors were buried there.

After the fire, plans were invited for the rebuilding and the great London architect Sir Christopher Wren was invited to prepare a design, which is now in the Wren collection. However, the plans of Sir William Wilson, a sculptor from Leicester, were accepted. Unfortunately, he did not appear to know the properties of the Warwick stone that he chose to use to build the tower. In 1700, cracks appeared and the tower had to be demolished to roof level and advice was sought from Sir Christopher Wren, who suggested that the tower should be built over the road. One wonders what Sir Christopher thought about his design being turned down, then being asked to advise on his successor's faulty one. It was decided to replace Wilson with Francis Smith and his brother William. Their design focused on the stability of the heavy stone and height of the tower and they used a local, hardwearing Shrewley stone. The west wall of the church was thickened to allow the tower to project over the roadway.

The new church was finished in 1704. You are welcome to go into the church and look round for yourself or take up the offer of a guide. There is much to see, including the chapel of the Warwickshire Regiment, with its evocative historical banners, several monuments to Warwick worthies and the Norman crypt. Most importantly, it also contains the Beauchamp Chapel. This houses the tomb of its builder, Richard Beauchamp, Earl of Warwick. It also contains those of Robert Dudley, Earl of Leicester, his son, the 'Noble Imp', and Dudley's brother Ambrose, Earl of Warwick. There is also some exquisite fifteenth-century stained glass. It was damaged during the Civil War and eventually reset, but not in the original design. Particularly interesting is the music in the glass high up on the north side. You will need a lot of time to enjoy another jewel in Warwick's crown.

*

St Mary's Tower.

Looking across from the tower, you can see the Old Square. This was a bold plan executed to replace the row of medieval houses and one narrow lane and make a grand space in front of the new church. Number 2, on the right hand corner, was the vicarage until the 1930s. Here is another use of Corinthian pilasters, the highest of the orders, and a very ornate doorcase.

On market days, the Women's Market extended along the narrow section of Old Square – no, not somewhere to buy women! By tradition, women would have run stalls selling chickens, eggs, and other light-weight produce. At one time two butchers, two drapers, a hairdresser and a solicitor were to be found as neighbours of a girls' school, a lodging house and a servants' agency.

On the garden across the road, to the left of the Old Square, once stood two houses that were demolished in the 1960s. A plan to build a road through to Swan Street never came to fruition. A plaque states that this garden commemorates the third millennium in Warwick.

*From the Church Tower walk to the right and
look up the elegant vista of Northgate Street.*

Before the Great Fire this became known as Sheep Street because the sheep were penned here on Market Day as there was no room in the square. After the fire, the sheep were penned in The Butts and the name gradually returned to the earlier name of Northgate.

This still-elegant street has been described as 'the most handsome Georgian Street in the Midlands' – this portrayal hides the fact that the houses are pre-Georgian, having

ROBERT DUDLEY, EARL OF LEICESTER (1531–1588)

Robert Dudley is best remembered as the favourite courtier of the first Queen Elizabeth. On her accession, he was made Master of the Queen's Horse, a prestigious position that required much personal attendance on the Queen as well as organising her public appearances, progresses, and her personal entertainment. He owned Kenilworth Castle, and on two occasions lavishly entertained the Queen, nearly bankrupting himself on the second. His brother Ambrose, who was created Baron Lisle and Earl of Warwick in 1564, owned Warwick Castle. They were sons of the once-powerful Duke of Northumberland, who had been beheaded for his part in the plot to usurp Elizabeth's sister, Mary, by putting his eldest son's wife Lady Jane Grey on the throne. Despite his dangerous family history, he was not averse to risking the Queen's displeasure. He married twice, first to Amy Robsart, who died in suspicious circumstances, and second to Lettice Knollys, Countess of Essex. Amy's death, and the fact that he married Lettice in secret, angered the Queen so much that she banned him from court for a year. Leicester's lifestyle was expensive and he was not liked by many of his fellow courtiers, who said he was arrogant and greedy. Leicester understood the importance of public image, so the charitable buildings such as Lord Leycester Hospital would underline his piety and charitable works. His tomb in the chapel, and those of his brother, his second wife and his son, are placed very close to that of its founder, their ancestor Richard Beauchamp. This emphasises their dynastic heritage to the Beauchamp line, rather than their troublesome Dudley connections.

Old Square.

Northgate Street – east side.

been built within three years of the Great Fire. Perhaps the description includes the two great public buildings on the west side and reflects some eighteenth-century decorations. The houses on the east side were the premises of the Warwickshire Education Service from 1905 to 2006.

Cross the road and walk to the far end of the first stone-built building.
Turn to face Number 6.

Number 6 is the best example of what the post-fire houses would have looked like. Built of locally produced brick, it shows the architectural requirements to the letter. Most of the other houses have been rendered, reflecting their owners' desire to emulate more luxurious stone in order to impress onlookers with their taste. Notice the thick barriers to the right, designed to look like pilasters, which make a sturdy division between the houses as a fire precaution.

The houses were homes to the wealthier tradesmen and gentry of Warwick, thus fulfilling one of the purposes of the Act of Parliament. However, in the 1840s Warwick County (the forerunners of the County Council) gradually began to buy them as they became vacant. Numbers 8–14 were occupied by officers of the Militia, and in 1847 the archway was made and buildings 'to store arms, accoutrements, clothing and other military requirements' were erected in the gardens.

Walk up the road and stop outside the entrance to the Shire Hall.

Numbers 18 and 20 used to be an inn called The Green Dragon. This must have been a very smart place to stay if you were visiting Warwick, perhaps for court business or the pleasure of the races. As the town became more gentrified, neighbours may have frowned on the activities of the inn, wanting their street to convey a more residential air. By 1775, it was sold and divided into two private houses. There is a very attractive window in the attic, the glass of which looks unmatched. It has been suggested that there are two rooms with one window, but there is only one attic room covering the two houses and a previous occupant installed an opening, probably to let in fresh air.

The family next door were probably most relieved when the public house closed. Number 22 is the most imposing house in the street and was the home built by Francis Smith for his family. It was built of stone, and the style and choice of materials underline his growing importance as a citizen of Warwick. A further reminder of his status is the stepped entrance, the only one in the street, serving as a visual reminder of his elevation in Warwick society.

Cross the road and stand outside Number 16.
Turn and face the buildings across the street.

You can now see the three public buildings that have attracted many admirers of eighteenth and early nineteenth-century architecture.

The Judge's Lodgings, to the left, were built in 1814 as the official residence for travelling judges who presided over the courts at Shire Hall. The building is in the neo-classical style popular at the time, with horizontal rustication of the ground floor, a tall first floor and a Greek Ionic porch. The architect was Henry Hakewill, the architect of the Gothic buildings at Rugby School. The cost was £8,000.

In the centre is the grandest building in the street. This is the Shire Hall, and until December 2010 the premises of Warwick Crown Court. The first building on this site was called the Steward's Place. It is recorded in a deed of 1480 but may have been older. In it, the Earl presided over the Manorial Court. By 1571 it was known as the Shire Hall,

No. 6 Northgate Street.

Attic window – 18–20 Northgate Street.

No. 22 Northgate Street.

where the Assizes and Quarter Sessions were held. By 1680, it had been repaired and refronted. During the fire of 1694 a team of thirty men who were paid to fight fires managed to save it, but there is no evidence why. Perhaps there were valuable historical documents and regalia, the loss of which would have been unthinkable.

In 1747 the Justices decided to rebuild and approached Sanderson Miller, a gentleman architect who lived at Radway, a village in south Warwickshire. He employed William and David Hiorn who, after the death of Francis Smith, had become the principal builders in Warwick. It was completed by 1776.

This building reflects the thinking of mid-eighteenth-century architects faced with a public building of such significance as the courts of justice. It uses all the elements of the classical Roman style that Robert Adam had made fashionable. Miller used composite capitals as a reminder of the building's noble purpose and the rustication is a statement of strength. A band of swags decorates the whole length of the building and in the pediment, as the crowning glory, is the Warwickshire coat of arms and motto. The imposing central bay with its niches surrounding the entrance door also gives prominence to the building. The visual impact of the building emphasises the importance of its function – justice! The Shire Hall is a public statement, emphasising the confidence and knowledge of those who designed and built this grand edifice.

Being the county town, the Assizes were held in the Shire Hall four times a year and these drew in even more visitors, who came to see the colourful procession of the judges, watch the prisoners enter the courts and wait with noisy excitement for the

Shire Hall.

verdict. Just as popular were the Quarter Sessions, bringing in all the JPs from round the county, traders, and those needing licences for business or leisure, and sightseers who enjoyed watching the minor felons brought to justice.

In December 2010, these activities came to an end. The Courts Service has moved to Leamington and will no longer deal out justice from this beautiful building. No decisions have been made about the future use, leaving 'the most handsome street in the Midlands' uncertain of its future.

Nikolaus Pevsner, the architectural historian, described the Shire Hall as 'festive', contrasting the building next door as sombre, almost sinister. As the new County Gaol, it was deliberately meant to look plain. Until new prison premises were constructed in Cape Road, prisoners were taken from here to the court next door to pay for their crimes. Built by Thomas Johnson in 1777–83, it has been greatly admired by architectural historians and said to be 'at the cutting edge of the next phase of public building design'. Although a local architect, he had obviously studied the designs of the great Frenchman, Claude-Nicolas Ledoux. It is one of the earliest attempts to adapt Greek Doric to the purposes of an English public building.

However, in several respects it was found that Johnson had failed to comply with the terms of the contract. One complaint was the columns of the façade had not been fluted 'as intended'. Another was that the brick partitions in the interior had not been carried up to the height of the roof 'by way of security'. Johnson claimed the justices

Gaol.

had not wanted the fluting, but he was obliged to reduce his fees for other work he had not carried out.

The Doric pilasters and portico were chosen deliberately to reflect the purpose of the building. This may have been the first example of the use of the Greek Doric Order on an English public building, which is an indication of the confidence and forward thinking of the Justices of the Peace. There is an octagonal vaulted chamber underneath, constructed in 1680, which replaced what was described as 'a dark close hole or Dungeon under Ground where they [the prisoners] had not Room to lie down one by another'. Prisoners were still put in this dungeon as late as 1797, and in the garden behind there is a grim reminder of the dungeon, covered by an iron grating.

This rather overpowering building perhaps was intended to intimidate the prisoners who were marched through the entrance. As these poor men and women looked up, they would have seen a carving of chains and manacles over the door. This dire reminder of the discomfort facing them has been removed. In the twenty-first century, prisoners who arrived regularly in the white van for their trials at Warwick Crown Court were not incarcerated in this grim prison habitation from previous centuries. There is one more feature of this once formidable building that you will come to shortly.

By 1861, the prison was becoming overcrowded and a new one was erected near the Cape, an area named after a public house called The Cape of Good Hope, which is on the canal, to the north-west of the town. As part of the alterations to the old prison, three arched openings were put in the central portico. The interior buildings were

Shire Hall Dungeon.

Doric capitals.

demolished and replaced by barracks for the Warwickshire Militia. When they moved out to Budbrooke in the 1930s, the County Council took over the site.

Walk to the end of Northgate Street and stop on the corner.

Facing you is Northgate House, built after the fire about 1698. They are the earliest semi-detached houses in Warwick, and two of the earliest in the country. The two houses make a dignified end to a very elegant street. Timber-framed houses once stood on this site, some with thatched roofs, going to the left, but an earlier fire in the 1660s destroyed those up to Number 18, the black and white cottage that you can see down the hill. The Puckering family, who lived at the Priory, created a garden on the ruins, known as the Burnt Garden. After the fire, they built these houses as residences for two gentlemen. The building is a fine example of a late seventeenth-century style with eleven bays divided by a central carriageway, above which is a sundial. There is another one round the corner in Cape Road, dated 1698. This is an original sundial but was purchased by the present owner's grandfather, the architect Edwin Francis Reynolds, in the 1920s. Can you see where the builders have blocked the windows in order to mount the sundial on its pedestal? The bell at the back of the house came from the Priory after its demolition in 1927. This house is the only private residence in the Northgate area. Its neighbour was for many years the premises of Warwickshire County Council Staff Club. Recently refurbished, it is now Northgate House Conference Centre.

Northgate House.

Down the hill to your left is Saltisford, where the salt way came into Warwick. Before the days of refrigeration, salt was essential to preserve food. Warwick's supply came from Droitwich, the most important centre of salt production in the Midlands. Saltisford was once a busy, bustling suburb where many of the small traders lived and worked. It was refurbished during the 1980s and is now mostly houses and flats. Looking above the houses, you can just see Warwick Racecourse.

The County Buildings on your right were erected in 1883, and were the headquarters of the Warwickshire Police until 1945. Until December 2010, it was used as offices for the Court Services. Just round the corner into The Butts is the Punchbowl Inn. Opposite, you can see the present Police Headquarters on the corner of Cape Road, built in the 1960s. The land beyond is Priory Park, once part of the huge estate belonging to The Priory.

The Warwick County Record Office is built on part of the foundations of this once great and beautiful building, which was relocated to Virginia, USA in 1926. Warwickshire archives were kept at the Shire Hall, but as the historic documents and collections increased and many more researchers came to visit, space was at a premium. In 1973 they were transferred from the Shire Hall to a new building. In 2000, the building was refurbished with the aid of a £1.3 million grant from the National Lottery. It is now even busier with researchers mining the rich repository of history contained in its strongrooms.

Punchbowl Inn.

In the wall on the side of the old County Gaol, you will see a seventeenth-century cell door replaced after the fire and used until 1861.

Cross the road and walk along until you are opposite the blocked doorway.

The walls opposite are the original walls of the Gaol and Debtors' Prison. The only break in the plain walls is the huge doorway, now blocked, framed by pilasters and a huge cornice. This was part of the extension built by Henry Couchman in 1790–3. It has been recorded that this is where the public hangings took place. You can see the loops in the pilasters at each side and the hole at the top. These were used in setting up the scaffold in the days of public executions. One can imagine the crowd gathering on these days, jostling together in this narrow street, perhaps eating and drinking food purchased from the many stalls, waiting the appearance of the doomed felons. Brought out blindfolded to face the jeering crowd, the condemned would await the final words from the chaplain, after which silence would fall. The hangman would pull the rope and the felons would feel the jerk of the noose tightening about their necks as the fearsome power of the law despatched them into the next world. This exciting pastime for the public ended on 27 May 1868, when the last public hanging took place.

The area to the right was called Joyce Pool and the street was called the Bridewell, after the infamous Bridewell Prison in London. In 1663, Joyce Pool House, a beautiful Jacobean building, stood on this site, and until the area was demolished in the 1970s there were several streets of Tudor and later cottage-style houses.

Where the library now stands was the site of the Women's Prison. This was quite a large complex, with its own Governor's House, kitchens, malt house, day rooms, two exercise yards and a chapel. The whole area was cleared in the 1960s and replaced with this County Council office block and car park. Since the 1980s, the ground floor has been the premises of the County Library.

Walk along Barrack Street, cross the road at the end, and then walk down the ramp steps into the Holloway. [Disabled visitors should turn left here and enter the Market Place. Turn right until you reach the other end of the Holloway.]

The sign explains that there once ran a medieval road that was cut through the rock to ease the gradient for carts coming to the market place from Saltisford. It was crossed at this point by an iron bridge, erected in 1804.

In the Holloway, on the right, there are offices called The Clink, behind which was the site of the original Theatre.

At the end turn left – this was once the Pig Market – you are in Market Place. Stand by the statue.

This large open space adds to Warwick's charm for inhabitants and visitors alike. When the weather is fine there is a continental atmosphere, with the various hostelries putting their chairs and tables out for customers to enjoy the attractive surrounds. While relaxing with refreshments, you can admire the architecture of four centuries. Although the shops and offices have been much altered on the ground floors by the requirements of modern businesses, you can see the upper storeys have retained some of their original features. Look up and note the windows, chimneys and decorations that

Old cell door.

Execution Doorway.

Joyce Pool House.

indicate the style of the buildings. You will also notice the modern tile decoration on the side of the modern building adjacent to the steps. This was a project undertaken by 2,000 children in Warwick state schools in 2000.

The statue commemorates Randolph Turpin (1928–1966), Britain's first black boxing champion, who won the World Middleweight title in 1951. On the corner, behind the taxi rank, there is a modern stone building with four square columns. This was the site of the Corn Exchange. Next door was Whittiker's Fish and Chip Shop, whose owner, Jack Whittiker, was an amateur bantamweight boxer. He was not very successful, so turned to promoting and hired the Corn Exchange to put on boxing shows. Randolph, his brothers, and other local lads honed their skills inside and were rewarded with bags of chips if they lost and full fish suppers if they won.

Market Place reflects the original purpose of a market and a gathering place for the inhabitants of Warwick. The earliest charter to hold a market was given in the thirteenth century and a market is still held every Saturday. The attractive detached building facing you is the Market Hall. The business of the market was originally controlled from the Booth Hall, built near the same site, but by the 1660s it was becoming the worse for wear. A subscription fund was raised to replace it on the same site with the present building, and in 1670 William Hurlbutt, a local carpenter and builder, was invited to build a new hall.

The Market Hall is a good example of a public building of the late seventeenth century. It is built in local sandstone, with a large and overhanging roof. The arcades were originally open for market stalls, and below ground floor level is a small lock-up used until 1848 for felons awaiting trial. This windowless cell serves to remind us of the tough treatment of those who brushed with the law. The elegance of the building was probably lost on them – impressed on their memories would be confinement and despair.

Market Place.

Right: Randolph Turpin.

Below: Market Hall.

In 1836, the Warwickshire Natural History and Archaeological Society created a museum in this building, and it was during the Victorian era that the arcades were enclosed. By 1932, the Society could not afford the upkeep and offered it to the County Council. Demolition was discussed, but fortunately nothing happened until 1962, when it was restored and it is now a very fine museum. Along with all the other exhibits, there is also a model of Warwick before the Great Fire, which would help you to imagine those earlier centuries.

The building now occupied by The Tilted Wig was rebuilt after the Great Fire and the front façade changed in the eighteenth century to a butchers' market. The arches would have been open. Today, the whole area is clean and neat, but one can imagine the scene when the butchers were carrying the carcasses into the covered area, cutting them up, piling entrails on the floor, letting the blood run down until some young lad was ordered to sluice the mess with buckets of water. Among all this housewives, intent on a bargain, would be arguing with the traders for a good price.

For centuries, the annual Mop (or Hiring Fair) took place here. Servants wanting to leave their present employment would stand in groups, waiting for prospective employers to offer them work. They would hold the tools of their trade. Housemaids would hold mops, thus giving the name to the fair. You can imagine the crush of people and get some idea of how crowded and exciting it would have been with everyone milling round – some looking for bargains, others meeting friends and, adding to the general mayhem, children racing up and down.

The concrete building on the north side represents the mid-twentieth century's interpretation of public architecture. The Shire Hall was designed by Eric Davies, then County Architect, built in 1966 and opened by the Queen Mother. It is attached on the

Mop Fair – Market Place.

Abbotsford.

right to a brick section built in 1957 by C. R. Barnsley. These buildings, modernist in style, allow you to consider how they fit in with the traditional designs and whether they create a homogeneous vision. If you walk up to the Shire Hall, you will see the delightful sculpture that Warwick Council commissioned to celebrate the Millennium. It was designed and created by Rachel Higgins, a young Warwickshire sculptor. The theme of wildlife, three herons catching fish, offers a touch of the countryside in this busy market square.

To end your visit to the Market Place with what is suggested to be its most stunning building, look at the very beautiful house in the north-west corner. This is Abbotsford (previous page), said to have been built by Francis Smith for his father-in-law, Job Lea, in 1714. Smith used his favourite motifs of scrolls on either side of the main window and pilasters framing the whole house and the very grand doorway. It was once part of a row of houses, but alterations to the Market Place detached it until the County Council constructed a bridge when the house was restored and provided further office space for the council. Restored again in 2006, it is now private apartments.

Turn round and leave the Square with the Shire Hall on your left. Walk to the top of New Street and stand on the corner opposite the Coffee Tavern.

From here, you can appreciate the grandeur of St Mary's Church Tower, soaring into the sky in the elegant setting of the Old Square.

This corner also illustrates three different Victorian architectural styles. The Coffee Tavern was built in 1880 on the site of two houses. Its purpose was to encourage people to meet friends, play dominoes and billiards, or just socialise, in an alcohol-free environment. Alcohol had brought health problems and financial ruin to many of the working classes and the Temperance Movement was making huge efforts to turn people away from drink. It was opened in 1881 by Lord Leigh of Stoneleigh Abbey. The Warwick Band of Hope, one of the many groups affiliated to the Temperance Movement, played at the opening ceremony in front of many local notables, including Alderman Dale, a partner in the Nelson Dale gelatine works, who generously covered the cost of £3,000 for the building. The architect, F. H. Moore, a local man, was obviously an admirer of the popular fashion for decorated terracotta tiles. Notice the amount of detail, all with fussy patterns, the wavy line of the cills and the machine-made tiles. The Commissioners who regulated so strictly the rebuilding of Warwick in 1694 would turn pale at such fanciful extravagance.

Six years later, the Coffee Tavern changed its purpose and became the Dale Temperance Hotel, with seven bedrooms on the top floor to help reduce losses. By 1939, it had become the County Council staff club.

The Old Post Office, next door to the Coffee Tavern, was opened in 1887 on the site of four houses. The architect worked at Her Majesty's Department of Works and it was built by William Robbins, a local builder. It reflects an earlier popular style of Victorian architecture, which copied features and decorations from the medieval Gothic style.

On the opposite corner, across the road, the attractive arched windows in the building on the corner capture your attention. This reflects the owner's interest in Venetian Gothic. There is nothing quite like them in the rest of the town. The effect is somewhat quirky and it seems to have attached itself to the house in New Street in the spirit of playfulness.

Walk along New Street.

Number 3 is a very attractive house with a unique frontage. It had been rebuilt after the Great Fire but by the mid-eighteenth century, perhaps the owner wanted a more individual look amid the regulated uniformity of the rest of the rebuilt town. The bust in the niche is a classical-style head, which has been placed in the niche within the last thirty years. The identity is a mystery!

St Mary's Church.

Coffee Tavern.

Old Post Office Doorway.

Venetian-style windows.

Carry on down New Street, and immediately after the car park you can see on the left a fine example of a timber-framed house built in the late fifteenth century, since faced with brick and render. On the corner of New Street, there is a little block of seventeenth-century timber buildings that escaped the fire. The house on the corner was built in 1634. Although it has been restored, it is a fine example of a Stuart town house, three storeys separated by jetties. Although it would not have been black and white, the timber framing is original but the lath and plaster infill has been replaced by brick. Can you find the three carved heads above each other on the corner of the house? One is called Old Tom. He and his companions were raised to prevent them from damage by passing traffic.

At the end of New Street you have reached the Corn Market, with Swan Street to the left. Under the pavement to your right were Victorian lavatories, now covered over. You never know what is under your feet!

Opposite these half-timbered houses is Brook Street. Cross over and walk down.

Brook Street used to be called Cow Lane because cows were penned here when it was market day. Lord Brooke had the name changed in the 1790s, but since then the 'e' has been lost. Past the houses, a mixture of traditional styles with adaptations and modern offices, tucked back on the left side stands Brook Hall. In the 1750s, a small

Old Tom.

Houses on Corn Market.

Congregational group broke away from the parent church in High Street and had a chapel built on this site in 1758. It has been enlarged several times, and the current building was constructed in 1826 after a design of Thomas Stedman Whitwell, who incorporated the plain, stuccoed Regency-style front. It is now a private office.

Cross over on the corner and go down Puckering's Lane,
named after the family who owned the Priory.

Opposite you can see the school once called Westgate County High School, now flourishing as Westgate Primary School. It was built in 1884, but the builders have reflected examples of Warwick's attractive architecture with some floral plasterwork in panels above the doors. On the site of the school was a bowling green that belonged to the adjoining hotel, but now contains flats.

Turn left along Bowling Green Street.

On the right there is a road called Friars Street, and the house on the corner of Bowling Green Street and West Street is called Friars House. An order of Dominicans established themselves in Warwick in 1263. In England and other countries, the Dominicans are referred to as Black Friars because of the black *cappa* or cloak they wear over their white habits. The friary formerly stood further down Friars Street and an alleyway still exists between the houses and out onto West Street, which originally served the friary. The present house was built on the site of three medieval house plots in the nineteenth century.

Westgate School.

You are walking just outside the line of the medieval defences, and if you look to the left you may be able to catch glimpses of the old wall as you make your way to the West Gate. On the left are Guild Cottages built by the Charity of Thomas Oken and Nicholas Eyffeller in 1992.

When you reach Westgate, turn right and look down West Street. This street leads onto the Stratford Road and has always been the main road to Stratford-upon-Avon. The buildings cover a range of architectural styles that have developed piecemeal over the centuries. No cataclysmic event forced a sudden change on these homes! The Victorian terrace opposite Blackfriars House, above Castle Lane, is modest in fashion, with a cornice of machine-cut bricks just adding a touch of decoration. The building below Castle Lane, with the idiosyncratically placed porch, was once a public house called the Malt Shovel.

The row of houses further down appear to be eighteenth century, but behind the brick frontage there are earlier timber-framed buildings. West Street has a number of examples of houses with different periods of timber framing, including Tinkers Hatch (part of a 'Wealden' house) and Park Cottage, which lay just outside the town.

From here, you can also see the pretty spire of the Church of St Mary Immaculate. In the nineteenth century, there was a strong revival of religious faith in the Roman Catholic Church. Warwick's first Catholic church was designed by Edward Welby Pugin (1834–1875), who was the eldest son of A. W. N. Pugin, a famous architect and designer of Neo-Gothic architecture. St Mary Immaculate was one of a hundred Catholic churches he designed. In 1916, the marriage took place between J. R. R. Tolkien, the author of *Lord of the Rings,* and Edith Mary Bratt. Tolkien was a devout Roman Catholic and Edith's family were against their relatonship. However, Edith wanted to marry him and moved to

Guild Cottages.

The Former Malt Shovel Inn – Westgate.

Tinkers Hatch –West Street.

Warwick in 1913 to stay with a relation in Victoria Street. In his poem 'Kortirion Among the Trees', Tolkien wrote of a town on a hill with lots of trees and a river flowing at the foot of the hill. He stated that the inspiration for this town on a hill was actually Warwick.

Turn to look at West Gate.

In the Middle Ages, Warwick was a safe, secure and defensible town – at least in principle. If you look to the left of the gate, across the corner of the garden, you can see some of the town wall surviving underneath the Lord Leycester Hospital. The tower is about fifty feet high and, helped by its position on a hill, would have soared over its surroundings. But look at the narrow opening of the gate itself. Now the road is quite wide and the traffic charges round the gate, but originally everything had to squeeze through this tight gap. Imagine what this would be like on market day with an impatient crowd of people, with their carts and animals, pushing and shoving to get into town. And they say congestion is bad now!

Just to the left of the gate are some almshouses built against the cliffside of rock forming part of the town wall. They were built in 1889 by Louisa and Julia Harris in memory of their mother, Louisa. Their father had been a Master of the Hospital. The present ones are on the site of almshouses for eight poor women, which were founded by the Warwick Guild and supported by a charge on the Priory estate.

Walk through the town gate.

This gate was built in the fourteenth century and was called 'Hongyngate'. As you walk through, look at the foot of the walls on either side. You can see the bare sandstone on

St Mary Immaculate.

Alms Houses – Westgate.

which Warwick is built. This has not been worked by masons; it is natural rock that the builders of the gatehouse have used to give added strength to the defences of their town. Now look up at the roof. In contrast to the unworked rock, here the masons have carved stone to create an elegant yet powerful ceiling. This is a ribbed groin vault with carved bosses where the ribs meet.

As you emerge from the gate you will see a Victorian post box, one of a pair, the second one being situated at the East Gate. They were put in place in 1856. Notice the fluted Doric column design, a reminder perhaps of some of the classical motifs that you will see around Warwick.

You are now standing in High Street, or High Pavement, as it was known in the Medieval and Tudor times.

Walk up to the end of the railings.

Turn and look at the large half-timbered building beside you. This is one of the most famous buildings in Great Britain, the Lord Leycester Hospital. It is open to the public and is well worth a visit.

Lord Leycester Hospital.

Before 1413, two Warwick Guilds (Holy Trinity and the Blessed Virgin, and St George) combined into the United Guilds. They built a Guildhall here and rebuilt the fourteenth-century chapel that they had been granted. The Guilds were dispersed in 1546. During the 1560s and 1570s, Warwick School had premises in here.

In 1571 Robert Dudley, Earl of Leicester, acquired the site and founded a hospital (or hostel) to provide homes for twelve old and infirm soldiers or seamen. They were called brethren and were overseen by a master. The hospital was run on the terms of the original charter until 1956. The charter was repealed but the purpose of the hospital is still accommodation, and today eight ex-servicemen and their wives live in modern and comfortable lodgings. They attend services in the chapel every day. Above the gateway you can see two shields – on the left the two-tailed lion of the Dudley family and on the right the De L'Isle arms. Lord De L'Isle is the patron of the hospital.

Until the twentieth century, the buildings to the right of the hospital's gate were not part of the hospital. The building next door, the former Anchor Inn, is one of the most important of the surviving sixteenth-century buildings in the town. The two-storied porch has a decorated framework, including carvings of flowers. The decoration is a provincial version of fashionable motifs, including flowers, scrolls and classical brackets. You will see the rear of this building shortly.

Across the road are three houses that escaped the Great Fire. Number 45 was built in about 1450, although part was rebuilt about 1600. Behind this house is where the Great Fire started on 5 September 1694. The owner, Mr Joshua Perkes, was a baker by trade, but not using the premises officially. There were several barns at the south-west corner of his property, in which were stored coal, hay and brush to the value of £8. It is not known how the fire started, but the event was exacerbated by three unfortunate facts. It had been a hot day, the west wind was blowing strongly and the contents of the barns were highly inflammable material. The flames took hold quickly and spread along the next two gardens to the rear of the Friends' Meeting House and, gaining strength, it destroyed the whole building and so on down the street.

With a little imagination, this view gives some idea of how Warwick looked in the centuries before the fire of 1694.

Walk up to Brook Street and turn left and walk into the entrance
of the Lord Leycester Hospital car park.

Find a good place to look at the back of the hospital. This was also the back of the Anchor Inn. The section that juts out from the rest was originally the brewhouse. The half-timbering with its elaborate patterns is an indication of the wealth of its owner, Sir Robert Dudley, who was never one to hide charitable works. Its survival was fortunate and its visual style appealed to the Victorians, who copied it. You can see the pattern appearing in other buildings around Warwick, which were actually built later than you might think.

A delightful contrast to the medieval architecture is the modern sculpture of the bear and ragged staff, another piece of work by Rachel Higgins.

Cross over and walk back down the road towards the main street.

Just before the corner, look at the exposed beams of the buildings on your right. If you look very carefully you can see a few traces of a reddish colour on the wood. Contrast this wall with the striking black and white of the house opposite Lord Leycester's Hospital, on the other side of High Street.

The Victorians thought that half-timbered buildings should be black and white. You can see several examples of black and white timber decoration in the town. However, this would have surprised the original owners of the houses. Their houses would have had muted shades of cream, red and brown, and you see faint touches of red which have survived for over 400 years. Lime was added to the paint to combat insect infestation.

Look across at the Friends' Meeting House (The Warwick Quaker Centre).

The local Quaker group may have begun after a visit of the founder, George Fox, who came to Warwick in 1655 and 1656. One Quaker was imprisoned in 1658, and those who opened their shops on Christmas Day 1660 were attacked. Fox came to visit several of his followers who had been imprisoned in the gaol. Such was the feeling against them that 140 were in the gaol in 1661 and between twenty and forty in 1666. However, by 1671 their presence must have been accepted and they were able to buy a house on the site behind the modern building you can see for their meeting place. Unfortunately, it was one of the first buildings to go up in the flames of 1694. The house was very quickly rebuilt in 1695, and the brick building at the rear illustrates that the Friends wished to keep some of the original features. The house was closed in 1909, reopened in 1949 and from 1954 was again in use for regular worship. The present building on High Street was erected in the 1990s. The main principle of peace and quiet is reflected in the topiary garden and graveyard, which can be reached by the side entrance where you can find the original 1695 meeting house.

Former Anchor Inn.

Tudor Houses – by Westgate.

Bear in Lord Leycester Hospital Garden.

1695 Quaker Meeting House.

Walk left along the High Street.

The first two houses on this side were not destroyed by the fire. The planners required that they were altered externally to suit the new architecture after the fire. Inside there are medieval timber frames. At the end of the first three houses, note that there is a break in the building line and the frontages are then in a straight line to Church Street. This is where the fire crossed and destroyed houses in its path right down to Jury Street.

Continue along, then stop opposite the Unitarian Chapel.

The line of seventeenth-century houses is broken by the Unitarian Chapel. The congregation were originally Nonconformists, or Presbyterians, who met at a house in the grounds of the castle. As part of the Earl of Warwick's plans for the extension of his grounds, he gave this site in exchange. This chapel was built in 1781 and enlarged in 1863. It is in the Gothick style with gable ends of stone ashlar. Gothick is an eighteenth-century version of medieval gothic.

Continue along High Street.

This section of the street reminds us most clearly of the vision the post-fire Commissioners had of their town. They required elegance and regularity and demanded that owners conformed to set rules which are well illustrated in this street. These included prescribed heights, building materials, dormers and windows. As you walk along, look out for these recurring features.

Some of the houses have retained their original façades over the centuries while some owners have enhanced their houses with decorative features, such as fanlights, shell door covers, rosettes or an oriel window that pleased their personal taste.

Outside Number 30, pause to look down Back Lane on the opposite side of High Street.

Here is a glance into the hidden world behind the frontages. The wall at the end of the street reminds us that one of the most beautiful castles in England is a few steps away. Have a good look at Number 23, the large building on the corner of High Street and Back Lane. The regulations required by the Act of Parliament to rebuild Warwick have been carried out to the letter. It is larger than most others and looks very grand and serene. However, if you were to look at it from the back, you could see that part of the original house remains. Underneath the brick of the rebuilt house is part of an earlier timber building. It is suggested that the fire only destroyed part of this house, as in several others in the town, and that the unburned back walls were incorporated into the new house. This house is the premises of the Freemasons.

Although these were intended as homes, as the centuries passed some of the owners may not have needed the whole house or perhaps were required to rent out some of the rooms. Although education was not compulsory until 1870, those who could afford private education sent their children to school. The size of the houses lent themselves particularly to the practical requirements of a school. Number 36 was the premises of Miss Maria Hilton's School in 1874.

Walk to the corner of Swan Street.

As you are walking on, look across the road to see The Warwick Arms Hotel. This was formerly called the White Swan, named after the Swan Inn that stood on the other side of High Street before the fire (the one that gives its name to Swan Street). This building dates from the 1790s and was built by William Eborall, a Warwick mason.

From this point, you will notice that more of the buildings contain shops and businesses. This has been so since medieval times. Although the fronts have been modernised, merchants and shopkeepers have always used their premises for all sorts of commerce. However, after the fire dangerous trades were banned from the centre of the town. These would have included anything that required a large fire or caused extreme smells. A good example would have been a tannery. We can see that the requirement for elegance and the need to carry on a business have been successfully managed by the powers in charge of the town. The building that now houses the NatWest bank on the corner of Swan Street was built in 1924, replacing two eighteenth-century houses.

Continue down High Street to zebra crossing. Cross the road using the zebra crossing.

Number 3, at the end of the crossing, was once the home of Thomas Oken (*d.* 1573), a merchant and benefactor of the town. The house was rebuilt after the fire and now has a classical style doorway, rather dramatically painted in black. The symbols indicate that it was once the premises of a Masonic Lodge. The wood was carved from the beams and supports of the windmill in Birdingbury, a Warwickshire village, by T. H. Kendall, a member of the Warwickshire Woodcarvers, in the 1890s.

The Warwick Arms Hotel.

*Turn left and walk to the end of Castle Street. You are now back at the High Cross
and can continue the second part of the tour. Now turn right into Castle Street.
Walk down to the Dispensary.*

Castle Street has a mix of architectural styles, and on the right you will see that there
is an inscription detailing the foundation of the Warwick Dispensary in 1826. Included
in measures for the improvement of public health were provision for hospital and
medical facilities. The Warwick Dispensary for the sick and poor of Warwick and
its neighbourhood was opened in this building in 1826. Its funds came from public
subscriptions and the proceeds of an annual charity ball. The Revd E. T. Smith, vicar
of St Paul's, Friar's Street, founded what became known, after 1859, as The Warwick
Provident Dispensary. Twelve years later, a branch at Emscote was amalgamated with
these premises and a limited number of beds were provided. *The Victoria County
History* records that by 1900, there were five beds and a crib, and the average number
of in-patients was about fifty (possibly in-patients can be taken to mean day patients
– fifty patients in ten beds would have been a tight squeeze). With the introduction of
the National Health Service in 1948, the Dispensary closed its doors.

THOMAS OKEN (*d.* 1573)

Thomas Oken was a well-to-do merchant and great benefactor of Warwick in the sixteenth century. He was a mercer, a trader in cloth, spices and other goods, and joined the guild and became a respected member. By 1545, Oken was Master of the Guild and owing to his status and business experience, he became mayor of the new Corporation. His will reflects his desire to help the poor of Warwick by provision of almshouses, annual income for the residents, and distributions of money to the needy. Almshouses were built in Pebble Lane, but were destroyed by the Great Fire. In 1696, replacements were built next to those of Nicholas Eyffeller at Backhills. Oken funded a schoolmaster's post to teach poor children, and money for a learned schoolmaster for the grammar school. He left money to St Mary's for a small choir of children and payments for sermons to be read. Money was allotted to repair the fabric of the town and its amenities, including the services of a beadle to clean the Market Place and streets adjoining High Cross, and to expel vagabonds from the town. It even included payment to a herdsman to keep the poor people's cattle on the common. He also left money to pay for festivities, and one feast that is still celebrated takes place at the Lord Leycester Hospital towards the end of January each year. Finally, he left his silver plate to the Corporation and surplus funds were to be used, if necessary, to pay for soldiers for the Queen's wars – a charge usually paid by the townsfolk. Thomas Oken died in 1573 and has been remembered as a great benefactor to his town. Sadly, he and his wife had no children. Warwick remembers him as a Tudor philanthropist who cared about his town and its people and sought to do them good in perpetuity.

Castle Street.

The Dispensary.

The building has been refronted to reflect its civic dignity as a public Dispensary. However, if you look up to roof level you can see that the later work hides a late seventeenth-century post-fire building revealed in the dormer window. You will also notice a fire plaque on the central dormer. This represents the badge of the fire company with whom the house owner was insured and who would respond to a fire. If you had a fire, only the company with which you were insured would attempt to put it out.

At this point, turn and look up to St Mary's Church. This vista was the subject of a drawing of 1740 by the Italian painter Antonio Canaletto, who was staying at the castle. Although now more busy, it is still a very attractive view.

Further down on the right, Number 10 Castle Street was originally built about 1500, as you can see from the half-timbering, although it has had later alterations. In 1626, this and another house were given by their owner, David Price, to provide income for one of his charities.

Another great benefactor built the delightful Tudor house, which, no doubt, has captured your attention as soon as you entered Castle Street. This is Oken House, owned by Thomas Oken. Regrettably, it has been much altered and refaced. The building has been put to many uses. In 1790, the Countess of Warwick established a School of Industry for girls between eight and fourteen. The original numbers were about sixty and it must have been very crowded. The school moved to Number 9 in 1823 and survived until 1882.

Take a few minutes to walk round the house and you can get a sense of how narrow the medieval streets were before the fire. It is quiet now, but imagine the scene 350 years ago, the townspeople bustling about their business, stopping to talk to each other, pressing up against the walls in order to let others pass. Greetings may have been called from upstairs windows, adding to the general hum of voices and animal noises.

Walk down further and stop outside Number 24.

Across towards the castle wall there are examples of fifteenth-, sixteenth- and seventeenth century houses on two sides of a small square. One has been modernised, but the others are more or less faithful to their original design. The wall ahead makes an abrupt end to Castle Street. This was a result of the earl's extensions to his grounds in the last decades of the eighteenth century and was built to prevent people from using the old way to the original bridge through the castle grounds. Notice that the road here still retains the cobblestone surface, which is the typical surface of a road in the eighteenth century. This may have been repaired, but has not been resurfaced.

Fire Mark.

Canaletto's view –250 years on.

Thomas Oken's house.

Walk to the end and turn right. Bear left towards the castle entrance. Go through the Town Gate in the castle wall. This gate is available when the castle is open to the public. Warwick Castle Management welcomes you walking through and hopes you will visit the castle after you have completed this tour. [If you are a disabled visitor go straight down Castle Lane to the main road and turn right. Continue along the side of the wall until you come to Mill Street.]

Although the castle is a magnificent building, there is little chance to get a view of it when walking round the town. On this path you are rewarded with two excellent views. The first is through the gate to your right. This was probably the continuation of the old footpath from Castle Street.

Continue through the castle reception area, turn right and walk along the gravel path, over the wooden bridge and down the stone steps.

At the bottom of the stone steps, look through the iron gates on your right. Here is another magnificent view of the entrance, guarded by the stunning towers of Guy's Tower on the right and Caesar's Tower on the left.

Continue walking left to the end of the path.

You are walking through a section of the foundations of medieval Warwick! The original town was built directly on the rock. This sunken lane was cut out when the new road and bridge were constructed in the 1790s.

Exit through the Castle Lodge gate and turn right into Mill Street.

This once very busy street and main thoroughfare to the south is now a charming cobbled cul-de-sac. As you stroll to the end, take time to notice the different styles of architecture from the early medieval through to late Victorian. Perhaps the other streets in Warwick would have looked like this had the town not suffered from the Great Fire.

It is difficult now to work out on maps how people arrived at the bridge. One way was to continue along Castle Street, then around the end of the present eighteenth-century stables (which replaced earlier houses) and round on to the top of Mill Street via a narrow passage. The alternative, if you had wagons, was out through Eastgate, turning right down Gerrard Street, then down Mill Street to the Great Bridge.

The last building on the left, just below the castle tower, is Mill Cottage. Here is one of the most beautiful small gardens in England, and it is worth a visit now for three reasons. Firstly, to enjoy the peace and beauty of this delightful garden; secondly, to see the remains of the old bridge; and finally, it allows you to enjoy one of the most splendid views in the country – a close-up view of the castle from the river and the overwhelming sense of power created by Caesar's Tower. You can also see the foundations upon which the castle is built and understand why the king chose this site for his castle in 1068. There is a small entrance fee to the Mill Garden.

Mill Street.

Doorway – Mill Street.

Ruins of Old Bridge.

Return to the top of Mill Street. Turn right.

Walk down and stand on the new bridge built by the earl in 1794 and enjoy another of the most stunning and awe-inspiring views in England. For six hundred years, this noble castle has stood solidly on its tall cliff, guarding the ancient town of Warwick. It was a constant reminder of the powerful earls who lived within its walls. Sir Walter Scott called it 'the fairest monument of ancient and chivalrous splendour which yet remains uninjured by time', and on sunny, bright days, with the river sparking below, it continues to thrill the viewer.

At the end of the bridge is Bridge End, a quiet road with some interesting architecture.

When you have had your fill of this magnificent view, walk back to the Castle Lodge Gate of Warwick Castle.

Across the road is St Nicholas' Church Street. On the corner, you can see the second of Warwick's parish churches, built on the site of a nunnery destroyed by the Danes in 1016. Norman earls built the first church, from where, in 1695, the bells rang to welcome William III. The medieval church was rebuilt in 1779 by Thomas Johnson, the same man who built the County Gaol, and who quarrelled with the justices. There is no evidence of any falling out over this building! Most of the houses in the street

Warwick Castle.

Bridge End.

St Nicholas' Church.

have retained their Tudor appearance, and the Bowling Green public house was once a medieval hall house.

Continue up Castle Hill.

The wall on your left was built in the 1790s as the boundary of the Castle grounds. This area was changed almost beyond recognition when the new road was built. On the corner of Castle Lane, you can see the almshouses of Nicholas Eyffeller and Thomas Oken across the road. To the left is the new Baptist Chapel of 1998, which replaced the previous Victorian building.

At a convenient point stop and look across at the East Gate.

The original gate was built at the same time as West Gate. The present structure was built in the fifteenth century. The narrow entrance is similar to West Gate and the road has now been directed round it. The chapel on top is dedicated to St Peter, and replaces an earlier one that stood at the junction of Church Street and High Street. The present one was repaired and altered in 1790 by Francis Hiorn, in the Gothick style, and is much lighter in tone than West Gate.

Cross Jury Street at the traffic lights. Turn to your right and cross The Butts at the traffic lights. Stand under East Gate.

Note the second Victorian pillar-box in front of the gate. You can also glance up The Butts. In medieval times, all towns would have had an area for practising archery and these were called butts, after the targets at which the archers aimed. This area was halfway up the street, on the right. Until the end of the fifteenth/early sixteenth century this street was a cul de sac, the entrance being at this end. Note on the side of the first building on the right two sections of decorative Victorian tiles, similar to those on the Coffee Tavern in Old Square.

Eyffeller and Oken Alms Houses.

East Gate.

Victorian post box – East Gate.

Victorian tiles – The Butts.

Walk through East Gate and stop outside Landor House.

You are now at the top of Smith Street. You may wish to investigate this street when you have more time. It has been a busy commercial street since medieval days and the buildings display a good mixture of styles. Most of them have original walls that have been refronted over the centuries by their owners. Number 71 is a much remodelled Wealden-type house.

The splendid building on your left is Landor House. It was built for Dr William Johnson in 1692, before the fire, by Roger Hurlbutt, who designed the Market Hall in the Market Place. It reflects the domestic architecture of a wealthy owner in the late seventeenth century. This is a smart symmetrical house, emphasised by two wings on either side of a recessed centre section. It is built of brick with stone corner quoins. The enriched modillion cornices and a very decorated doorcase draw attention to the wealth and taste of Dr Johnson, and the steps use the device of elevating the social level of his family. Passers by and neighbours would have been impressed.

It was fortunate that in the aftermath of the fire, the planners had only to walk down to this house to study the most up-to-date architectural style to give them the basic design for the rebuilding. No doubt Dr Johnson was very pleased, as he had made himself very unpopular by his actions during the fire. Horrified by the relentless march of the fire down Jury Street, he persuaded the mayor to order the demolition of Edward Heath's house there in order to create a firebreak. Without the consent and 'much against the good will' of Mr Heath, his house was taken down, but it was at this moment that the fire suddenly changed direction, thus prompting criticism of Dr Johnson's hasty action. The Fire Court agreed with Mr Heath and decreed that Dr Johnson should pay him £20 in damages.

When Dr Johnson died, his widow left the house as an endowment for a charity and the trustees let the house to the Landor family. The poet Walter Savage Landor was born here in 1775. King's High School for Girls took over the house in 1879 and gave the house his name as a mark of honour.

This is a good place to envisage what Warwick was like before the fire and probably until the nineteenth century. Smith Street has been in existence since medieval times and has always been a busy shopping area. Just glance round and feel the atmosphere and imagine that the cottages came right up to the East Gate. Remember standing outside West Gate? It would have been a similar scene here in past centuries, with queues of people and animals, carts piled high with produce or materials, all jostling to get into the town, especially on market days. Imagine the noise and the smell!

At the bottom of Smith Street is St John's House, which is now used as a museum for social history and the Warwickshire Regiment. In origin this was a medieval 'hospital'

Landor House.

Modillians – Landor House.

that, after the dissolution of the abbeys, became an ordinary house and was rebuilt in the 1660s by Anthony Stoughton. This is a lovely town house set in landscaped grounds, and is one of the few houses of the Jacobean period left in Warwick.

Return though Eastgate and cross back to Jury Street.

The street is named after the small community of Jews (i.e. Juerie or Jewry) who lived in Warwick from about 1180 for 100 years. They had gone by the time Jews were actively expelled from 1290, but their memory lives on. The Fire did not affect this lower part of Jury Street, so the houses have been adapted during the centuries to reflect the owners' choice of fashion. Most have new facings or added details.

The first house on your right is a medieval house, although it is wearing a disguise. It is probably the oldest of seven medieval timber-framed houses that survive within the traditional walled area of Warwick. The present front dates from 1856. Again, the colours reflect the Victorians' misinterpretation and may have been done to make the house seem more theatrically Elizabethan. The superficial paint surface is the same as the style of the Anchor Inn brewhouse. The larger wooden beams are real, the smaller ones are fakes. Unfortunately, this makes the whole image look artificial. It was once the home of the seventeenth-century physician James Cooke, author of *The Marrow of Cururgery.*

The building next door, once called The Porridge Pot (a reference to Guy of Warwick), is also very old, probably a fifteenth-century, three-bay medieval house since covered

St John's House.

House in Jury Street – still being updated.

NICHOLAS EYFFELLER

Nicholas Eyffeller was born in Westphalia, an area of Germany east of Cologne. He was brought over by Sir Thomas Lucy, the builder of Charlecote, to work on the glass of his newly built house. Eyffeller lived in Warwick in 1568, first near the Market Place but then moved to Jury Street (where No. 18 now stands). Apart from his business as a glazier, he adapted part of his house as a tavern and was registered as publican and maltster. He was head of a small German colony in Warwick with whom he was related and he leased a small house on Jury Street for his brother-in-law, John Goldsmith, to live. Like Oken, he and his wife had no children. His wife gave a place in her home to a poor beggar boy. They were active in the relief of poverty of the people of Warwick and after the poor harvest and grazing problems of 1586, Eyffeller helped thirty poor people by allowing them to graze their cows on his meadows. In 1589 he bought a large house in Jury Street (on the site of No. 4), which he planned to be the principal endowment of his almshouse charity. In his will he left money for almshouses to be built, and these were completed in November 1597 as four dwellings under one roof, with four chimneys, four beds and four of most other fittings. It would have pleased both Oken and Eyffeller that their almshouses were legally united in 1957, are occupied today, and that their legacies of good will and kindness towards their town are still in evidence after more than four hundred years.

with a façade of brick and stone in 1700. Its original name was Bridge House, and it had been given to the town by Margaret Porter in 1568 so that its rent might help to pay for the maintenance of the Great Bridge.

The large house on the opposite side of the street is called Eastgate House. Further along, there are two ornately decorated timber-framed houses. A house on the site of what is now Number 14 was the home of Nicholas Eyffeller, whose almshouses you have just seen on Castle Hill.

Walk up Jury Street.

The fire had reached the house that is now the Lord Leycester Hotel when the wind changed direction. Behind the present façade is what remains of a much older stone house in Jacobean style. It was the town residence of the Archers of Umberslade, a very old Warwickshire family, and it remained in their ownership until the end of the 1700s. By 1820, it had been bought and divided into two. The one on the left was the Three Tuns Inn, which was demolished in 1832. It is now the Lord Leycester Hotel, which was opened in 1926.

On the opposite side of the road there are a few more timber-framed buildings that the Victorians improved! Note that the width of the footway in the middle of the street is wider than at the ends. This is a feature of this street, and High Street had the same feature before the Great Fire. The reason for this is not known but in other towns with similar features, it is believed that the wider areas were used for market purposes.

The Three Tuns – Jury Street.

Continue up Jury Street to the corner of Church Street.
You have now completed the tour.

I hope that you have enjoyed this tour of one of the most handsome towns of England. Fire is a terrible hazard, but it is known that out of the ashes a phoenix will rise. From the ashes of a seventeenth-century near disaster, far-sighted planners helped to create a town that is unique in England. It is a priceless inheritance to the inhabitants of today and to those of the future and we hope you, as visitors, will return again and again to enjoy its fine architecture, the rich tapestry of history, the beautiful gardens and the friendly welcome from the townspeople.

PICTURE CREDITS

St Mary's before the fire	PV.WAR.St.Mar.4
Joyce Pool House	PV.WAR.Joy.1
The Three Tuns	PV.WAR.Jur.2
Shire Hall Cell	PH143/1142
The Old College	PV.WAR.Col.4
Poster for Lion Fight. 1825	Z818(sm)
Mop Fair, Market Place	PV.WR.Mar.5
Barrack Street	F4212 (@D1865)

The County Record Office standing on the site of The Priory
By kind permission of Warwickshire County Record Office

Map – by kind permission of Rosemary Booth

Elephants in Jury Street   W.C.R.O. Holte Collection PH1155
Fire Mark – Rosemary Booth
Bear and Ragged Staff – Rosemary Booth
Portraits of Francis Smith, Nicholas Eyffeller by kind permission of Derek Maudlin, Town Clerk, Warwick Town Council.

Photograph of Bear in Lord Lycester Hospital Garden by kind permission of Jennifer Meir.

Photograph of attic window – 18–20 Northgate Street by kind permission of Tony Brown.

Photograph of Randolph Turpin by kind permission of Denise Greenhalgh.

All other photographs by Richard Cluley.

Portraits of Lord Brooke and the Earl of Warwick by kind permission of Warwick Castle.

Many thanks to my husband, Richard Cluley, for all his photographs, and for his encouragement and support.

ACKNOWLEDGEMENTS

I would like to thank two people in particular, without whose help this book would not have been written: Steven Wallsgrove, for generously sharing his knowledge of thirty-five years of delving into the Warwickshire archives, and Gillian White, whose excellent editorial skills and constant support are much appreciated.

I am grateful to the staff of Warwickshire County Record Office for their support and kindness, especially Mark Booth, Robert Pitt and Nadeem Janjua.

I am also grateful to the following people for their help: Rosemary Booth, Julie and Tony Brown, Richard Chamberlaine-Brothers, Richard Cluley, Julia Dowle, Susan Grey, Christine Hodgetts, Andy Kilgour, Colin Jones, Derek Maudlin, Richard and Veronica Phillips, Maria Poulton, Shirley Wallis, Warwick Library Coffee Group, and Compton Verney Social Group. The quote from correspondence between Earl of Warwick and Capability Brown from Pakenham Correspondence has been used with the kind permission of the British Library.

FURTHER READING

Richard K. Morriss & Ken Hoverd, *The Buildings of Warwick* (Stroud, Alan Sutton
    Publishing, 1994)
Michael Farr, *The Great Fire of Warwick* (Dugdale Society, Hertford, Stephen Austin &
    Sons, 1992)
Andor Gomme, *Smith of Warwick, Francis Smith, Architect and Master-Builder,*
    Stamford, Shaun Tyas, 2000)
Richard Chamberlaine-Brothers, *Notes on College (Unpublished)* W.C.R.O. Z502(sm)
Charles Lines, *The Book of Warwick* (Barracuda Books, 1985)
Edmund Bealby-Wright, *Warwick* (Birmingham, Sketchbook Guides, 1994)
Jack Turpin and W. Terry Fox, *Battling Jack*
Mainstream Publishing Company (Edinburgh) Limited, 2005
CRO - C920 TUR
Joan D. Browne, Shirley Wallis, Steven Wallsgrove, *The Past In Warwick*
Christine M. Cluley, *Northgate Street,* (Warwickshire County Council) 2005
J. R. R. Tolkien, Kortirion Among the Trees
Victoria County History

BUILDINGS OPEN TO THE PUBLIC

These buildings have their own guidebooks and guides. These can be obtained from
Tourist Information Office in the Court House.

COLLEGIATE CHURCH OF ST MARY
Old Square
Tel. 01926 493940
Famous for the Beauchamp Chapel
Admission – free but voluntary contributions are welcome.
Tower – admission charge.

LORD LEYCESTER HOSPITAL
High Street
Tel. 01926 491442
www.lordleycester.co.uk

The Queen's Own Hussars Museum is situated in the hospital.
Admission charge

WARWICK CASTLE
Tel. 0870 442 2000
www.warwick-castle.com
Admission charge

MUSEUMS

WARWICKSHIRE MUSEUM – MARKET HALL
Market Place
Tel. 01926 412500 or 412501
www.warwickshire.gov.uk
Admission Free

THE QUEEN'S OWN HUSSARS MUSEUM
(See entry for Lord Leycester Hospital)

ST. JOHN'S HOUSE MUSEUM
Coten End
2 museums

1. St. John's Museum (Warwickshire Museums)
   Tel. 01926 412132 or 412021
   www.warwickshire.gov.uk

2. Royal Regiment of Fusiliers Museum
   (Royal Warwickshire)
   Tel. 01926 491653
   www.warwickfusiliers.com

Admission Free

WARWICKSHIRE YEOMANRY MUSEUM
The Court House
Jury Street
Tel. 01926 492212
Admission free

WARWICKSHIRE COUNTY RECORD OFFICE
Priory Park
Cape Road
CV34 4JS
Tel. 01926 738959
Email: recordoffice@warwickshire.gov.uk
www.warwickshire.gov.uk/countyrecordoffice
(see page 93)

GARDENS

The Master's Garden
Lord Leycester Hospital
Tel. 01926 491422
www.lordleycester.co.uk
Small admission charge

Pageant Gardens
Small public gardens
Castle Street
Admission Free

The Mill Garden
Mill Street
Tel. 01926 492877
Small admission charge

The Quaker Garden
High Street
Tel. 01926 497732
Admission Free

The Unitarian Chapel Garden
High Street
Admission Free

College Gardens
The Butts – or entry from St. Mary's churchyard
Admission Free

St. John's House Garden
Tel 01926 412132 or 412021
www.warwickshire.gov.uk
Admission free

Hill Close Gardens
Bread and Meat Close (off Friars Street)
Tel. 01926 493339
www.hillclosegardens.com
Admission charge

St Nicholas Park
Banbury Road
Tel. 01926 494743
www.warwickboats.co.uk

Warwick Common
Priory Park

PLACES TO STAY IN HISTORIC WARWICK

Warwick Arms Hotel
High Street
Warwick
CV34 4AT
Tel. 01926 492759
www.warwickarmshotel.com

Lord Leycester Hotel
19 Jury Street
Warwick CV34 4EJ
Tel. 01926 491 481

And finally – when you get home try out this recipe to remind you of your visit to Warwick.

WARWICK PUDDING
50g (2oz) glacé fruits
650ml (1¼) pints milk
½ tsp ginger
25g (1oz) gelatine
3 egg yolks
3 tbsps rum or brandy
3 egg whites
a little butter
100g (4oz) caster sugar

Serves about 6

Butter a mould or soufflé dish of about 1 litre (2 pt) size. Then decorate the bottom with the chopped glace fruits.

Heat up the milk, and beat the egg yolks. When the milk boils, cool a little, and then strain the egg yolks into it, whisking all the time. Add sugar. Dissolve the gelatine in a little warm water and stir until it is quite dissolved. Add to the custard.

Set aside to chill until it is beginning to set, like the consistency of raw egg white. Meanwhile, whisk up the egg whites until very stiff. When the custard is ready, fold them in carefully so they get down to the bottom. Add the rum or brandy. Pour into the dish carefully, trying not to disturb the fruits. Chill to set. Turn out by wrapping a hot cloth around the dish, putting a serving plate on top and turning over quickly.

WARWICKSHIRE COUNTY RECORD OFFICE

Unique historical resources available for everyone

WARWICKSHIRE'S HISTORY, WARWICKSHIRE'S MEMORY

Safeguarding, managing and developing Warwickshire's archives so that they can be accessed, interpreted and enjoyed by all those with an interest in Warwickshire's Past and its People.

If you have enjoyed this book, and would like to learn more about Warwickshire's heritage, carry out your own research using original archives dating back over 900 years, or take part in our events and activities, please contact us.

Warwickshire County Record Office (in colour) stands on the site of the seventeenth-century priory (in grey).

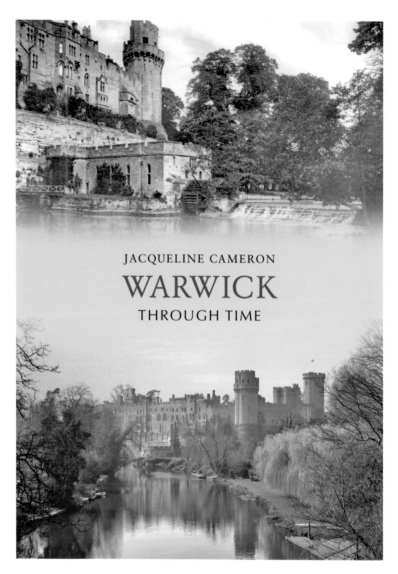

JACQUELINE CAMERON
WARWICK
THROUGH TIME

Warwick Through Time
Jacqueline Cameron

This fascinating selection of photographs traces some of the many ways in which Warwick has changed and developed over the last century.

978 184868 874 2
96 pages, full colour

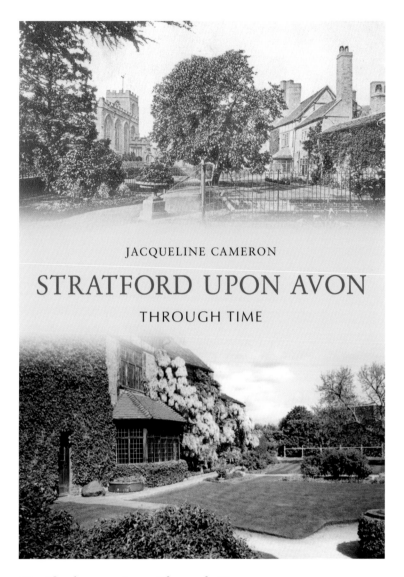

JACQUELINE CAMERON

STRATFORD UPON AVON

THROUGH TIME

Stratford upon Avon Through Time
Jacqueline Cameron

This fascinating selection of photographs traces some of the many ways in which Stratford upon Avon has changed and developed over the last century.

978 184868 903 9
96 pages, full colour

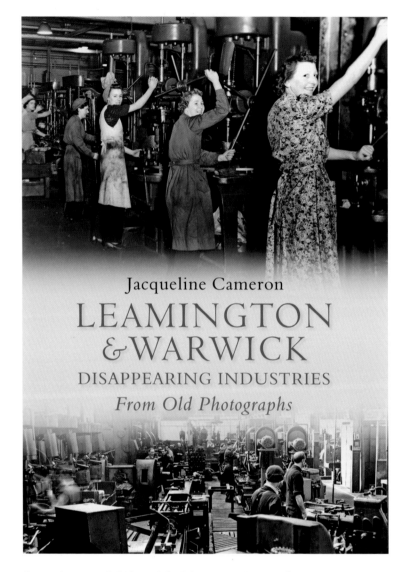

Jacqueline Cameron

LEAMINGTON & WARWICK

DISAPPEARING INDUSTRIES

From Old Photographs